Sugar Was
My Best Food
Diabetes and Me

Carol Antoinette Peacock
Adair Gregory
Kyle Carney Gregory

illustrated by Mary Jones

Albert Whitman & Company
Morton Grove, Illinois

For Our Deep and Enduring Friendship.
—K. C. G. and C. A. P.

For My Friends.
—A. G.

Thanks to Paige and Claire.
—M. J.

Library of Congress Cataloging-in-Publication Data

Peacock, Carol Antoinette.
Sugar was my best food: diabetes and me / Carol Antoinette Peacock, Adair Gregory, and Kyle Carney Gregory; illustrated by Mary Jones.
p.   cm.
Summary: An eleven-year-old boy describes how he learned that he had diabetes, the effect of this disease on his life, and how he learned to cope with the changes in his life.
ISBN 0-8075-7646-8 (hardback)   ISBN 0-8075-7648-4 (paperback)
1. Diabetes in children—Juvenile literature. 2. Diabetes—Juvenile literature. [1. Diabetes. 2. Diseases. 3. Gregory, Adair.] I. Gregory, Adair. II. Gregory, Kyle Carney. III. Jones, Mary, ill. IV. Title.
RJ420.D5P43   1998   97-27869
362.1'9892462—DC21   CIP   AC

The design is by Scott Piehl.

Thanks Go to the People Who Helped Me

Dad, Mom, and my brothers, Stephen, Connor, and Quinnie—my family, side by side.

Mrs. B. and Larry—you took such good care of me, from the time I was small.

My fourth- and fifth-grade teachers, Polly Wagner, Heidi Lyne, and Mrs. Cataldo—you helped me get through those first rough years.

Dr. Gerald Hass, my pediatrician; Dr. Lori Laffel, Acting Chief of Pediatrics at the Joslin Clinic, Boston; and Paula Michel Fanizzi, my pediatric nurse—you've been a great health-care team.

P. S. Thanks also to Keven Wilder, my grandparents, all my aunts and uncles, Michelle and Lynda, Dianne M., and Slugger.

Contents

Chapter 1

Just a Normal Kid

My name is Adair. Adair means "courageous and strong" in Irish. Two years ago, I got diabetes. This is the story of how I got sick and how I got better.

I'm eleven years old and I live in a town near Boston. I'm tall and skinny and I have blonde hair. I like sports—I always have, even when I was a little kid. I'm a good runner. I like to sprint, especially near the finish line. I'm the pitcher on my dad's Little League team. When I grow up, I want to be a pro-athlete.

I have three brothers. Stephen is the oldest—he's thirteen. He looks a lot like me, and sometimes people think we're twins. This kind of gets to Stephen, because he wishes he was taller. When we were little, he taught me how to chew bubble gum, how to ride a bike, and how to ice skate and get up when you fall. Most of what I can do I learned from my big brother. We share a bedroom on the third floor of our house.

Then comes me. Next is Connor, who is six. He's sort of loud and wild. We have a little baby brother, too, named Quinn. He thinks I'm really funny. If I just look at him, he laughs.

Of course, there's my mom and dad. Everybody in my family is Irish. Even though we're Irish, we eat mainly Italian food, like linguine with pesto, because that's what Dad cooks, and he's a really good cook. Oh, and we have a dog, a Kerry blue terrier that Stephen and I named Slugger. Actually, he isn't blue—he's black. We also have a canary named Paprika. For the longest time, I was trying to teach Paprika how to say "Polly-wanna-cracker" and my name, A-dair Greg-o-ry. Then Stephen told me canaries can't talk.

So about how I got sick. I was just a normal kid and we were going to Wyoming to visit my uncle's ranch. It was right after school got out. I was nine then. We were on the airplane, and I started to feel really gross. I thought I was going to throw up. It was like having the flu, only much worse. Mom thought I was airsick and kept giving me those paper bags they have for people to throw up in. Dad said probably I had a twenty-four-hour bug. Nobody guessed it was the Other Sickness.

Well, the twenty-four-hour bug didn't go away. At

the ranch that first day, I tried to ride my favorite horse, Gus, but I got too tired. When I went fishing with Stephen that afternoon, I thought I was going to pass out. And all the time, I was really thirsty. I stayed thirsty even after I drank gallons of water. It was like I'd swallowed a sponge.

By dinner, I had to lie down because I was so weak. While I was lying on the couch, I heard Mom and Dad talking about me. Mom had that worried look, when her forehead gets all tight and wrinkled. The next day, Dad drove me to the hospital. I figured it must be serious because my dad was a medic in a war once, and he knows a lot about sickness.

At the emergency room, I was so bad off I went to the head of the line. The doctors  hooked me right up to IVs. I don't remember much of it because I felt half-dead. I was really out of it. I couldn't move, I couldn't talk. Somebody stuck a huge needle in my arm to take blood to be tested.

Dad sat by me in the emergency room. He says he felt like he waited forever. Then the doctors came back. They told Dad that I had diabetes. It sounded like this: DIE-a-bee-tees. So I thought I was going to die.

I stayed in the hospital for three days. Mom and

Dad took turns sitting up with me at night. Mom cried sometimes, when she thought I was asleep, and Dad looked beat.

During the day, the nurses kept coming in and telling me about the sickness. I didn't understand much of it. I was too scared.

The main thing was, they said I wasn't going to die.

Every few hours, the nurses pricked my fingertip to get blood for testing. They also gave me two shots of insulin a day, in my arms or the tops of my legs. I felt numb. I just lay there, waiting for the next prick or shot.

Pretty soon, one nurse taught my parents how to give me the shots, too. She used an orange to teach them. All I could do was stare at that  round old orange that was supposed to be me.

When I was a little more with it, the nurse showed me how to prick my finger myself. The pricking part didn't seem nearly as bad as those shots.

By then I had gotten some of the picture, and it wasn't good. I was going to have to get two shots a day for the rest of my life! Diabetes also meant I couldn't have candy like before.

I couldn't believe it! Sugar was my best food. I *lived*

for candy. My favorite candies were Charleston Chews, Star Bursts, Skittles, and Twix.

Halloween was my favorite holiday. The year before, I dressed up like a rap singer, and Stephen and I went all over the neighborhood. By the end of the night, I'd gotten a huge bag of candy, so big I had to carry it in my arms, like the way I carry my baby brother, Quinnie. Stephen and I dumped all the candy on the kitchen table. We stood there, stuffing our faces. When Mom came in, she said, "That's enough, boys, you'll ruin your teeth." But you could tell she wasn't all that mad because Halloween comes only once a year, and how bad is all that candy just for once?

I also love cakes. I loved my birthday cake. Every year, my mom would bake me a special mocha cake covered with chocolate sprinkles. She'd make little playing fields with licorice sticks and put plastic base-ball or soccer players on the top, on account of how I liked sports so much.

Before I got sick, Dad would take me to the North End in Boston every Saturday. After we bought fruits and vegetables at the sidewalk stands, we would go to Dad's favorite cafe. I would order hot chocolate and a cannoli, the kind with the frosting dripping all over. Dad would get a cappuccino, and we'd read sports

magazines together. I always liked the stories about how pro-athletes got started.

So here I was lying in the hospital, and the doctors told me that for now I couldn't have candy or cake or cannolis because of this diabetes disease. Something was wrong with my pancreas, they said. I didn't quite get it. But I was going to have to prick myself and get shots and hardly ever eat sweets and if I did, I would get thirsty and weak. How could I ever pitch for my dad's Little League or ride bikes around Fresh Pond with my big brother if that happened? How could I run track and sprint towards the finish line, really fast?

I felt like my life was over.

Chapter 2

Big Changes

Diabetes means big changes.

I got so sick, we couldn't even finish our vacation. The day we got back, we had an appointment at a big hospital in Boston for people with diabetes. Just my luck! Two hospitals in one week!

In the waiting room, I was pretty nervous. I flipped through a sports magazine to keep my mind off things.

"Hello, I'm Dr. Gagen." My doctor shook my hand. She was short and smiled a lot.

"I'm glad you're here, Adair. We'll check you out today, and next time I'll introduce you to your nurse and dietician. Now let's review the diabetes information, just to be sure you understand it all."

Dr. Gagen had a book with pictures. A cartoon kid was pointing out this part in the body called the pancreas, which looked like the tongue of a shoe, right under the stomach.

She said the problem for me was my pancreas. Because my pancreas was out of whack, my body couldn't handle food right.

Dr. Gagen went on about how when we eat, the stomach breaks the food down into sugar. That's what the body needs to live. Like how a car needs gas to go, I figured. According to her, this sugar, called blood sugar or blood glucose, travels through the blood on its way to all parts of the body.

I couldn't quite see how this had anything to do with the pancreas. But Dr. Gagen went on talking. She said that to use the sugar from food, the body needs a helper, called insulin. The pancreas makes the insulin you need.

Unless you have diabetes.

My pancreas wasn't making enough insulin, so my body couldn't use the sugar that was moving through my blood. That's why I got weak and tired all the time.

"We need to do the job your pancreas can't do," said Dr. Gagen. "We have to get insulin into your body with two shots a day."

Great, I thought. Those two needles a day! I'll never get used to that.

I asked couldn't we please try pills instead. Like aspirin, I suggested. Even that caplet kind would be fine by me.

"I'm afraid pills won't work, Adair," said Dr. Gagen.

She went on talking. She said that all day long, the blood sugar in my body went up and down like a yo-yo, depending on what I'd eaten and how much I'd exercised. The insulin shots would help keep the blood sugar steady. But just getting insulin wasn't enough. It had to be the right *amount* of insulin so that the blood-sugar level would be as even as possible, hopefully between 70 and 180.

To find out exactly how much insulin I needed at each shot, I was supposed to stick my fingertip and check the amount of sugar in my blood. That reading would tell me how much insulin to use.

It sounded pretty complicated.

"Adair, are you listening?" Mom asked.

"Uh-huh," I said. "Steady levels."

Dr. Gagen went on. "Some foods— like candy—make that level way too high, even with the insulin shots."

There it was again, the thing about no candy. I was hoping they'd lighten up on that.

"We'll keep a close watch on you, Adair, especially in the beginning. You'll come here every three months for checkups."

I couldn't believe it! What kid in their right mind would want to go to the doctor so many times, for such a confusing sickness?

Dr. Gagen handed Mom a stack of papers. "Here's a list of all the foods Adair can eat, along with some meal plans."

"Meal plans?" said my mom. She looked pale.

It turned out those were combinations of foods that you had to eat at the same time. Why? You guessed it—to keep the blood sugar steady! Keeping those levels steady seemed like a big deal.

I sighed. My doctor touched my shoulder. "We'll get you feeling better first, Adair. I know your levels are all over the place right now, but after awhile they'll even out. Then, as long as you check your blood sugar and your parents give you insulin shots, you can pretty much eat what you did before. But you have to measure the amounts of food carefully and eat according to a strict schedule."

No pigging out, I figured. No skipping lunch because the ballgame runs extra innings.

As she said good-bye, Dr. Gagen gave me the book with the picture of the cartoon kid pointing out his pancreas.

I left the hospital with my head spinning. I sat by

Mom on the way home and closed my eyes. I felt faint and tired.

"Are you okay, Adair?" Mom asked. She pulled the car over to the side of the road right there on Storrow Drive. She grabbed the tester, and I pricked myself while the cars sped by. My reading was okay. I guess I was just beat from all the diabetes talk.

The amazing thing is, before the diabetes, I was never that into food, only candy. My mom always had to remind me to eat. After the diabetes, I cared about food a lot. So did my whole family.

We had to eat every meal on time. Before, we didn't even have a clock in the kitchen. Now we had a digital clock on the counter and a wall clock, too. My dad stopped cooking his most fancy Italian meals, except for on weekends. They took too long to make, and food had to be on the table by five o'clock or I'd throw my schedule off. And we never had ice cream or brownies for dessert anymore, only cantaloupe or boring sugarless jello. When we figured out that sugarless stuff sometimes gave me stomachaches, we even stopped the jello.

I had to eat three meals a day and three snacks, whether I wanted to or not. Even the snacks, which had sounded good at first, were a pain. I had to eat dry peanut-butter crackers or gingersnaps even if I wasn't hungry.

I could never sleep late on weekends because I had to be up by eight, check my blood sugar, have Dad give me my insulin shot, and eat breakfast. Before that, on Saturday mornings, my mom let me and Stephen sleep in. When I woke up, the sun would be coming through the curtains and my bed would feel all warm and cozy. Down in the kitchen, I'd make myself a stack of cinnamon toast, and then I'd curl up in front of the TV and watch all my favorite cartoons.

But not anymore. Now I had to get up to eat, and I kept eating, every three hours until bedtime. I also had to test my blood four times a day. To do that, I had to put a strip of special paper into my tester and prick my finger with this stick that looks sort of like a ballpoint pen except it's got a needle where the pen should be. Once I got the blood, I'd put a drop on the strip and get a blood-sugar reading. The reading told me if I was high or low. If I was high, I had to drink a lot of water and sometimes get an extra insulin shot. If I was low, I had to take sugar tablets or juice and also eat a snack to bring my level up.

My mom wrote down all the readings in a notebook

on the kitchen counter. The readings went way up to the two hundreds and way down towards fifty. This was bad, and I got very upset. Here I was, not eating sweets, having all these stupid pricks and shots, and my readings were off. No matter how hard I tried, I got bad readings. Why bother? Sometimes, when my reading was too high or low, I would get mad and scream.

"It's not your fault, Adair," my mother would say in her firm voice, trying to calm me down. But I didn't believe her.

Another thing about diabetes was, everybody worried. I worried, my parents worried, my brothers worried. My parents were always asking, "How do you feel?" or "What was your last reading?" or "When did you eat?"

There was so much worry in our house, I figured even Slugger and Paprika were worried. We were one big worry.

In the days right after the ranch, I was still very sick. I lay on the couch in the den, with my grandmother's soft blue comforter over me. I felt faint. Sometimes I felt like I couldn't even move. Lots of times I thought I was going to throw up.

My blood sugar just wasn't right. When I was low, I felt dizzy, and you could see my hands shake. It's scary

to see your hands shake right
before your own eyes. Sometimes
my hands shook so much I
couldn't even test myself. When
I was high, I got real thirsty, and I had to pee a lot.

I felt so weak, I couldn't ride my bike, I couldn't play basketball, I couldn't run. I didn't want to visit friends because I needed all those snacks and meals and insulin on time. I didn't want anybody to come over because I couldn't talk about what had happened to me. I just lay on the sofa and worried.

Nighttime was the worst. I'd lie in bed and wonder if my blood sugar was high or low. I'd start to think about how diabetes stinks. It made me so different, like I was weird. I'd get to feeling very lonely, like I was the only kid in the world with diabetes. Sometimes Stephen would hear me tossing and turning and he'd say, "It's okay, Adair," and he'd come over and throw his sleeping bag on the floor next to my bed. We'd lie there, side by side, all night long. I wasn't so worried when he was beside me like that.

My brother Connor was four when I got diabetes. He called it "die-a-bee-bees," like a BB gun. It sounded pretty cute. Every time I had a snack, he hopped up on the chair next to me and got a snack, too. He even liked those dry old peanut-butter crackers that nearly made me choke. When I drank a diet soda, he tried to get a sip. He *wanted* to have diabetes! Can you believe it? He'd walk around the kitchen saying, "Mommy, I have die-a-bee-bees. I have die-a-bee-bees, just like Dar-ie."

After about a month, Stephen got fed up with everybody giving me all the snacks and attention. He started saying that diabetes wasn't so bad.

"Really, Stephen?" said Dad. You could tell he was mad. "Okay, let's try it. We'll all go on Adair's schedule for a week to see what it's like."

Well, Stephen lasted a day and a half. He always seemed sort of nervous about pricking himself. He hated having to eat when he wasn't hungry, and he couldn't stand not eating candy whenever he wanted. I guess that showed him.

From the beginning, my mom had been calling the hospital every week to tell them my blood-sugar readings so she could figure out how to change my insulin doses. But no matter what we tried, my numbers were always too high and too low.

I still felt weak all the time. Even though I was eating all those snacks, I was losing a lot of weight. My mom said sometimes that happens when you first get diabetes. My shorts almost fell off when I walked. Sometimes my eyes didn't work right. Things would get real blurry, and I saw little dots wherever I looked.

I still had trouble falling asleep, and now Stephen didn't sleep beside my bed as much because I guess he was pretty sick of the diabetes. I overheard him telling Mom that I just wasn't the same brother anymore. He sounded kind of sad, the way he told her. I could tell she felt sad, too.

So I lay in bed after my last snack— it would be about eleven o'clock— and sometimes I'd go downstairs into my parents' room. Usually Mom was in bed, reading. She'd ask what was wrong, and I'd say I couldn't fall asleep. Then I'd start to cry about how hard it was to fall asleep, and I'd sob and sob.

"It's awful. The diabetes is just terrible," my mother would say, giving me a back rub or hugging me, when I let her. "It's okay to be scared."

"It's not that, it's just that I can't fall asleep," I'd tell her.

"I know. But I think it's the diabetes that's upsetting you," she'd say. Then she'd go on and on about how getting diabetes was so unfair, so hard. My mother is a social worker. Her job is to help people, which is what she was doing with me, even though I didn't know it at the time.

My father would do the same thing. He'd say, "It's awful. Awful."

If you have diabetes and you feel bad about it, it helps when people tell you that you're right to feel so bad. I don't know why this is, but it helped me.

Sometimes people say something like, "Oh, you have diabetes. Well, cheer up, they're working on a cure." When people said that to me, I wanted to puke.

Because maybe they are working on a cure, but if you have diabetes right this minute and you feel lousy, what good is a cure they haven't found yet?

By the end of the summer, we had gotten more used to the snacks and the readings and the shots. But there were so many changes it didn't even feel like my life anymore. The biggest change was me. I wasn't just regular old me anymore. I was a kid with diabetes now. That was the biggest and the worst change of all.

Chapter 3

This Fourth Grade Gets Snacks

The week before school, Mom set up a meeting with my fourth-grade teacher, Mrs. Wolcott. I'd had her for third grade, too—she was cool. The meeting was to tell her about the diabetes.

Mrs. Wolcott hugged me and said it was good to have me back, and then my mom said, "We came to tell you that Adair got diabetes over the summer."

When my mom said it, about the diabetes, Mrs. Wolcott hugged me even harder. Then we all sat down at the kids' desks, and Mom told her what had happened at my uncle's ranch. That was when Mom started to cry a little, and then Mrs. Wolcott was sniffling, too.

After the crying was over, we had the meeting. Mom explained that since Dad gave me my insulin shots before breakfast and dinner, I wouldn't need shots at school. We decided Dad would carry a beeper so Mrs. Wolcott could find him if I was really high or low. We also agreed that I would prick myself right in the classroom because I didn't want to leave to do it in the school nurse's office.

"He already feels so different," Mom told Mrs. Wolcott.

We decided that I would tell the kids about the diabetes right away so they wouldn't get scared or start making things up.

The first day of school, everybody had to say what they did over the summer. I told them that I got diabetes. Nobody said a word. Mrs. Wolcott said to tell the kids more about it.

So I told how my pancreas couldn't make enough insulin and you needed insulin to live. Then I told how I had to get insulin shots. To figure out how much insulin I needed, I had to prick myself and check my blood lots of times a day. I said I could hardly ever eat candy. The no candy part really got to them.

"No Snickers?" said my pal Chris. "You gotta be kidding!"

Some kids thought diabetes was another word for AIDS, and you could die from it. I said no, even though it sounded like DIE-a-betes, you don't die from it.

A lot of kids thought you could catch it, like chickenpox.

Mrs. Wolcott said no, they didn't know exactly what

made some people get diabetes, but you couldn't possibly catch it.

Sally said diabetes wasn't as bad as wearing glasses. You might have guessed—she wears glasses. I never could stand her. I told her no way, diabetes was much worse.

Nick said he had a learning disability, and maybe that was like diabetes. I could tell he felt bad for me, and that he understood my being sick.

At nine-thirty sharp, Mrs. Wolcott said it was snack time, which nobody could believe, because mainly you have snacks when you are in kindergarten.

But my mom and Mrs. Wolcott had decided that when I got my snack, the whole class would have a snack. That way, I wouldn't feel so weird.

Before the kids started their crackers, I got out my tester. Mrs. Wolcott said it was okay for the kids to watch, so everybody piled around my desk. I pricked myself until I got a drop of blood—no big deal. But some of the kids nearly passed out. They thought I was very brave.

"Come see Adair Gregory prick himself—he doesn't even blink," somebody said.

I felt kind of proud all of a sudden. Like even if I did have diabetes, I could do something nobody else had the guts to do. I was almost happy.

After about a minute, the tester showed my reading. The kids liked watching the numbers come up.

As time went on, we made it into a game. Kids would guess if my reading would be high, over 180, or low, under 70. Of course, I pretty much knew. Thirsty and tired and having to pee meant high. Dizzy and weak meant low.

When I got home that first day, Mom was waiting. She'd rescheduled her patients because she wanted to hear how my day had gone. I told her it was okay. That night she got a call from Sarah Fullerton's mother. Mrs. Fullerton told Mom that Sarah had come home crying because she was worried about catching diabetes. Now Mrs. Fullerton wanted to know the first signs of diabetes so she could tell if Sarah was catching it.

Can you believe it? I was in the kitchen, eating my snack, when Mom took the call. You could see her face turn all white, she was so mad.

Mom said, real cool, "As Mrs. Wolcott explained, diabetes isn't catching. You have nothing to worry about. And if Sarah is all that scared, you'd better talk with her further, because maybe there is something else bothering her.

"Diabetes is *not* contagious," Mom repeated, with little ice cubes in her voice, and then she said if Mrs. Fullerton had any more medical questions, she should call her own pediatrician and not trouble us at home.

Mom hung up the phone, and she was shaking.

"Good going, Mom," I said.

I felt really great because of the way my mom stood up to Sarah's mother. You should have seen her— nobody was going to push us around. If you are a kid and you have diabetes, sooner or later somebody will think they might catch it from you. Even my little brother Connor worried about it for awhile. The best thing to do is to say, really firmly, "No, diabetes isn't catching." Something like that. Try not to take it personally.

In school, we didn't talk that much about my diabetes after the first week or so. But I thought about it all the time. I couldn't pay attention to what Mrs. Wolcott was saying. When we colored in our explorers' maps, I couldn't even keep my markers in the lines— I was worrying so much.

Nothing made sense. I didn't get the math. I couldn't read our new reading book. I hated school. I hated the diabetes. I hated my life.

At night, I still couldn't sleep, thinking about how bad things were. Lots of times I went downstairs to my parents' room and yelled about it. Usually, after the yelling, I cried.

The only thing I liked about school was recess because we could run around. Also, it turns out, if you have diabetes, exercise helps keep your readings level. But sports were hard. When I got up to bat, my arms shook. When I played soccer, I kicked the ball out of bounds. I just wasn't good at sports anymore. How could I ever be a pro-athlete now?

My birthday came at the end of September. For our family party, Mom got a special sugarless cake at the bakery recommended by the hospital. We all sat down and took our first bites. It stunk. It was like eating cardboard. I yelled and stormed up to my room. That was how I turned ten.

After my birthday came Halloween. As you know, Halloween had been my favorite holiday. This year, I really dreaded it. I didn't want to go out—I couldn't face all that candy. So Stephen and Connor went trick-or-treating without me. I lay on the sofa and watched TV as if it wasn't Halloween at all. But the doorbell kept ringing. Every ring felt like a jab.

When Stephen and Connor came home, they ate

their candy in the kitchen the way Stephen and I used to do. The next day, Mom made them each pick ten pieces and throw the rest out. She told them it would be too hard for me to see them eating candy for weeks and weeks. So Stephen and Connor threw their candy in the trash. Boy, were they ever mad at me!

Right after Halloween, we had our school pictures taken. I got back a picture of a skinny kid with huge black circles under his eyes. I couldn't believe it was me. Even Mom sort of blinked when she saw the picture.

"It doesn't look like me— how I used to look," I told her.

"I know, Adair. It's still such a hard time." She said my readings were supposed to calm down after awhile. She said things were supposed to get better.

"When?" I asked her.

My mother put her arms around my bony shoulders and said she didn't know.

Chapter 4

Pretty Good for a Kid with Diabetes

Christmas was rough. We didn't have any candy canes on the tree—Mom got extra lights instead. But what's a Christmas tree without candy canes?

We didn't make our gingerbread houses, either. Every year before now, Stephen and I would make cool little houses out of graham crackers. We'd stick the crackers together with icing, and then we'd frost the whole house, like it was covered with snow. We'd decorate the houses with peppermints, red and green gumdrops, and chocolate kisses. One year, I figured out how to make fat little snowmen out of marshmallows to stand by the front door. We gave the houses to our baby-sitters for Christmas presents.

That year, instead of the gingerbread houses, we made our baby-sitters candlesticks out of beat-up old coffee cans. They didn't turn out that great.

In fourth grade we were studying Native American traditions. Mrs. Wolcott taught us how to make seed pots. To start, you get wet red clay and mold a pot, round but slightly squished, with a skinny neck for the plant to grow through. Then, with your thumbs, you push a hole in the top. If you want to make it look more real, you can sketch Native American designs around the sides while the clay is still wet. Mrs. Wolcott had a book showing all the designs and what they meant. I picked the signs for long life and healthy spirit.

Once the pot dries, you poke dirt inside the hole and put one little seed down there, too. The seed just sort of rests in that dark old pot until it is growing time. Then you pour some water through the neck and the seed sprouts. The plant finds its way up through the pot's neck to the sunlight.

I put a marigold seed in my pot and gave it to Mom for Christmas. After she unwrapped the pot, I told her how I made it out of clay from the earth, and I showed her the signs for long life and healthy spirit. Mom really liked that present. She kept it on her bureau beside our family photo.

Right after New Year's, Mom and Dad said they had a big surprise for us. Mom was going to have a baby! In the spring, the baby was born. A fourth Gregory boy! Like all the Gregory babies, he had a huge head and eyes round like an owl's. My parents named him Quinn, which is an Irish name, on account of how we're Irish.

I just loved that baby! Mom let me rock him in my lap and pat his big smooth head. On nice days, after I got home from school, Mom and I put him in his stroller and walked him in the park near our house. I held the handles tight and took long, steady steps so he'd get a real smooth ride. We took Quinnie out almost every day that spring. Each walk, we went farther and farther, even up hills. "To make Quinnie strong," explained my mom.

Sometimes when I held little Quinnie, I sang him Native American rain songs we were learning in school. I guess maybe I wasn't worrying about the diabetes readings *all* the time. I was too busy patting little Quinnie's bald head or pushing his stroller through the park.

Right around that time, Dad decided to train for next year's Boston Marathon. On Saturdays, I started running with him, around Fresh Pond. As the weeks went by, I felt myself getting stronger and stronger.

Mom was still keeping her charts of my readings with all the highs and lows. About the time I started training with Dad, my readings actually hit the right range once in awhile. One day we noticed that the readings had stayed okay—not too high, not too low—for three days. I thought, maybe I can go a week. I did!

Maybe we were finally getting the insulin doses right. Maybe, like Dr. Gagen had said, time had passed. That was supposed to help sometimes. Or maybe all that exercise was beginning to pay off. I don't know. But what I did know was that my readings were finally better, most days. Whew! What a huge relief for me.

In May, my parents let me sign up for town track. Track met every Wednesday after school. Most kids just  showed up with their track clothes stuffed into a sports bag. But I had to bring my three-thirty snack, my tester, and my sugar tablets, all in one sports bag. I also had to wear a chain around my neck with a medal that told people I had diabetes, in case I went low and passed out. I tucked the medal under my shirt because I didn't want anyone to see it.

Pretty soon we were getting ready for the town meet. By now, I could run really fast around the track. It was the first time since I got diabetes that I felt I could run like before.

The town track meet was held at the high-school field in June. It was a big deal. I was placed in the age ten-and-eleven group, and since I was ten, I was the youngest kid in that category. My mom and dad and brothers sat in the bleachers.

Before the race started, I patted Quinnie's head for good luck. The coach blew the whistle, and I was off. I could feel my diabetes medal banging against my chest. I ran as fast as I've ever run in my life.

I won.

They gave me a trophy in front of the crowd. Everybody clapped, and I felt really great.

Mom took a picture of me holding the trophy. I was grinning a great big huge grin. I didn't look so skinny, and the black circles under my eyes were gone.

I overheard Dad say to Mom, "I think we're getting our Adair back."

I qualified for the state meet, which was in July. The day of the meet, we were all real worried, because my readings were so high. It's bad to run if your readings are too high because you feel very tired. My mom kept having me test myself to check on the readings.

The meet was in the late afternoon. We all drove down to Braintree with Quinnie in the car seat. I tested myself right before the race started. Just

my luck—I was still very high. I felt thirsty and tired, but I really wanted to run anyway. Mom and Dad decided to let me try.

I went fast as an arrow.

When the race was over, I had come in sixth! That means I was the sixth-fastest ten-and-eleven-year-old runner in the state.

Pretty good for a kid with diabetes, huh?

Chapter 5

Even the Cook Had Diabetes!

That summer, Stephen and all my friends were going away to real camps, and I got stuck going to diabetes camp. I didn't even know there was such a thing! How much fun could it be? What kid would want to sit around all day and hear about the worst disease of their life?

Mom and I packed my clothes in my duffel, and I brought along all my Calvin and Hobbes books and my hockey stick. We had to drive an hour, clear out to Worcester. The camp was on a lake—it used to be an old loggers' camp. We slept in little log cabins with six kids each.

Let me tell you the most amazing thing about the camp. Everybody there had diabetes—all the campers, all the staff. Even the cook had diabetes!

This camp was real famous—there were kids from all over the United States, the world, even. We all had to eat at the right time, we all had to prick ourselves, we all had testers and readings. You would have felt weird at that camp if you *didn't* have diabetes!

My favorite counselor was Jonathan. Jonathan was in college, and he did sports, like me. He had a cool medical alert bracelet, like my medal, which he wore around his wrist. I decided I'd get one when I got home. Someday I want a medical alert bracelet with the word "diabetic" written in diamonds.

Anyway, Jonathan told me how at first he felt terrible about getting diabetes. He was thirteen when he got sick. But after awhile, he got used to the snacks, pricks, and shots, and he learned how to live without lots of candy and desserts. He could still do sports. He said his life got back to normal.

He didn't say that all at once. He just let me know, off and on, while we were getting ready for soccer or waiting in line for lunch or making bookcases at the arts and crafts lodge. I hung around with him because he was so cool.

The camp had classes about how to plan meals and eat healthy food. I learned that since my readings were more under control now, I could have a little candy and a few sugary snacks sometimes. If I was really low, I could have a cinnamon sticky bun, which was one of my favorite foods. At a birthday party, I could even have a small piece of cake, and not the sugarless kind, either. This was good news for me, as you know.

I also learned how to give myself my own shots, in case my parents weren't around. Jonathan and I practiced every day. He showed me how to measure the insulin and how to hold the syringe. Then he taught me how to pinch my skin with one hand and jab the needle into my arm or thigh with my other hand. By the end of the two weeks, I could give myself the shot with no problem. Like a pro, Jonathan said.

Now that I could give myself a shot, I might be able to go to dinner birthday parties or sleepovers at a friend's. I hadn't been to a kid's house longer than a few hours for almost a year. I couldn't wait.

The camp had its own radio station, and one day I got to be DJ. I announced all the songs. It was great to hear your own voice blaring all over the camp! At the end of the two weeks I got some certificates, for Canoe Wars, Best Bird-  house, and Watermelon-Seed-Spitting Contest.

I also got two awards, which were more important than the certificates. One award was "Good
Sportsman," which meant I didn't brag when I won
and I handled it okay when I lost. I also got the
"Cleanliness" award. Mom almost fell over when she
saw that because at home I am a real slob.

They had a little trading post at the camp, and
I bought a shirt with a picture of Elliott P. Joslin on
it. He was a doctor who was very big in the field of
diabetes.

The last day of camp, all the parents came to pick
up their kids. I said good-bye to Jonathan. He gave
me a high-five and said, "Stay cool."

Someday I want to be a counselor just like Jonathan.
Then maybe I can help some kid with diabetes get his
life back.

Chapter 6
Side by Side

For fifth grade, I had Mrs. Bolt. Mom and I met with her before school started so we could tell her about the diabetes. It turned out her cousin has diabetes, so she knew it wasn't catching and you wouldn't die from it and stuff like that.

It was great to see my friends again. The first week of school, Kevin Anderson invited me for a sleepover with a bunch of other kids from my class. I begged my parents, please, please, let me go. I reminded them how I could eat a little cake and give my own shot.

Mom called Mrs. Anderson. They had a long talk about snacks and having dinner on time and most important, about me giving myself two shots, one before dinner and one in the morning just before breakfast. Then Mom and Dad thought about it for a day. On Thursday, the day before the sleepover, they said yes.

Kevin asked me what I could eat, and he wrote it

all down on the back of his math
book cover so his mom could
buy the right things.

The sleepover was cool. We all
put our sleeping bags on the floor in the
basement and watched a Ghostbusters video. Around
five o'clock, we went upstairs so Mrs. Anderson could
watch me test myself and do my shot. The kids said it
was better than the video the way I pricked myself,
measured the insulin, drew it into the syringe, and stuck
the needle in my own arm. Nobody had ever heard of
any kid who could do that to themself. Especially the
shot. They all held their breath when I jabbed my arm.
Robbie had to sit down—he thought he was going
to faint.

One thing about diabetes: even if you don't give
yourself shots, kids will admire you and think you're
very strong. When I first got diabetes, kids used to
point at me, like at recess, and you could tell they
were saying, "See that kid? He has a bad disease." But
after kids in my class had watched me prick myself
for a month or so, other kids would come up and say,
"Oh, you're the kid who pricks himself. You must be
really brave."

I am.

The first thing we studied in fifth grade was Mexico. Mrs. Bolt said we could plan a Mexican party. She wanted to have a piñata, which is a hollow animal filled with candy. The kids in Mexico whack the piñata until it breaks and the candy spills out. Then they eat the candy.

The minute Mrs. Bolt started to describe the piñata, I felt nervous. Oh, great, I thought, candy. I started to feel like I used to—sort of weird and left out.

But Sam raised his hand and said, "No, we can't fill the piñata with candy because what about Adair?" And a lot of the other kids nodded their heads.

So they decided to fill the piñata with sugarless gum, sugarless fruit drops, little boxes of sugarless Tic Tacs, and bags of potato chips. They knew those were the things I could eat without even asking me.

We made the piñata out of papier-mâché in the shape of a donkey. We painted it bright colors, mainly orange and green. At the party, when it was my turn with the piñata,  Mrs. Bolt blindfolded me and I waved the stick, hard. I heard a loud whack and then a smash as the candy hit the floor.

I pulled off the blindfold and there were the kids, scrambling over the floor to get the gum and fruit drops and potato chips. They were jumping and laughing, they were so excited. I just stood there, watching them eat diabetes food. It was like we all had diabetes for a minute. I felt happy, and I smiled. Then I dove for the potato chip bag near my foot.

A few weeks later, my birthday came. I was eleven. Mom let me have a little slice of real cake this year, the way they'd taught us at camp. She'd made her special mocha cake with chocolate sprinkles. It was good to have that taste back again.

For my birthday, I'd asked for the diamond medical alert bracelet. It couldn't hurt to try. No such luck, but I did get a cool watch with an alarm that went off at my snack time.

Around that time, my mom asked me, did I want to do the walk for kids with diabetes? They have it at the end of every September. You collect money for the miles you walk, and the money goes for research to cure diabetes. Last year I'd been too weak and upset to go. But this year I said yes, I really wanted to.

I collected pledges from everybody in my class, and some kids that weren't even in my class. They'd just heard of me because of me being so brave and all. Mrs. Bolt and Mrs. Wolcott gave money. So did my baby-sitters—they've known me ever since I was born. Altogether, I got twenty-three dollars and thirty cents towards the cure of diabetes.

My whole family went on the walk, even Slugger. Stephen and I roller-bladed, and Connor rode his hand-me-down bike with training wheels. Mom carried Quinnie in a backpack. We wore tee-shirts that said, "Walk to Cure Diabetes."

Mom even put a tee-shirt on little Quinnie. It covered his baby slippers.

We all met at City Hall in Boston and walked through the Boston Common towards the Charles River. Then we went on Storrow Drive, right by the river. Stephen and I cruised along, weaving in and out of the crowd. Mothers and fathers carried babies in backpacks or pushed little kids in strollers. Many people carried balloons that bobbed up and down in the sky. Along the sidelines, volunteers at booths gave out sparkly water and peanut-butter crackers—things that kids with diabetes could eat.

Lots of families wore signs that said, "Betsy's Team" or "We're Doing This for Joe," who was probably their kid or somebody they knew really well who had diabetes.

Stephen and I went too far ahead for awhile, and then we turned back to find Mom and Dad and Connor and Quinnie.

Then we all walked side by side, the whole family. And what I knew was, they were doing this for me.

A Great Dream

Every year, my family and I do the Walk to Cure Diabetes. Each time, I say to myself, maybe this is the last walk. Maybe by next year they'll have found a cure. It can't hurt to hope.

Sometimes at night I have this great dream. I'm in the grocery store with Stephen, and I don't have diabetes anymore. I'm wolfing down Charleston Chews, Star Bursts, Skittles, and Twix. As you can guess, I'm in heaven. Then I wake up. I'm back to being a kid with diabetes.

Maybe someday soon a scientist will make a huge discovery that cures all kids with diabetes. But until then, if you have diabetes, it helps to know a few things. It gets better. The first few years are the roughest. Once your readings even out, you can eat pretty much anything, but in small amounts. Sugar is still my best food. I just don't get that much of it.

One more thing. When you get diabetes, you may feel like you're weird for awhile, and you may worry about what other kids will say. Don't hide your diabetes, but don't make a big deal about it, either. Just tell people, "I have diabetes, but you can't catch it." Kids who are your real friends will like you anyway. And that's what counts.

When I got diabetes, I felt really lonely. I didn't know any other kids with diabetes. That's why we wrote this book. If you want to talk to me more about your diabetes, I'd be glad to hear from you. Please enclose a stamped, self-addressed envelope. I'll answer every letter.

Adair Gregory
P. O. Box 207
Winchester, MA 01890